TSINTAOSAURUS
and Other Duck-billed Dinosaurs
by Dougal Dixon

illustrated by
Steve Weston and James Field

PICTURE WINDOW BOOKS
Minneapolis, Minnesota

Picture Window Books
5115 Excelsior Boulevard
Suite 232
Minneapolis, MN 55416
877-845-8392
www.picturewindowbooks.com

Printed in the United States of America.

Library of Congress Cataloging-in-Publication Data
Dixon, Dougal.
Tsintaosaurus and other duck-billed dinosaurs / by
Dougal Dixon ; illustrated by Steve Weston & James Field.
p. cm. – (Dinosaur find)
Includes index.
ISBN-13: 978-1-4048-4018-8 (library binding)
1. Tsintaosaurus—Juvenile literature. 2. Ornithischia—
Juvenile literature. I. Weston, Steve, ill. II. Field, James, ill.
III. Title.
QE862.O65D596 2008
567.914—dc22   2007040922

Acknowledgments
This book was produced for Picture Window Books
by Bender Richardson White, U.K.

Illustrations by James Field (pages 4–5, 11, 13, 15,
19) and Steve Weston (cover and pages 7, 9, 17, 21).
Diagrams by Stefan Chabluk.

Photographs: istockphotos pages 6 (Elijah Low);
bigstock photos, 10 (Steffen Foerster), 14 (Michael
Rolands), 16 (James Clark), 18 (Barbara Farfan), 20
(Nico Smit); Frank Lane Photo Agency 8 (Michael and
Patricia Fogden). Shutterstock photo page 12 (Joanne
Harris & Daniel Bubnich)

Consultant: John Stidworthy, Scientific Fellow of
the Zoological Society, London, and former
Lecturer in the Education Department, Natural
History Museum, London.

Types of dinosaurs

In this book, a red shape at the top of a left-hand page shows the animal was a meat-eater. A green shape shows it was a plant-eater.

Just how big—or small— were they?

Dinosaurs were many different sizes. We have compared their size to one of the following:

Chicken
2 feet (60 centimeters) tall
Weight 6 pounds (2.7 kilograms)

Adult person
6 feet (1.8 meters) tall
Weight 170 pounds (76.5 kg)

Elephant
10 feet (3 m) tall
Weight 12,000 pounds
(5,400 kg)

TABLE OF CONTENTS

WHAT'S INSIDE?

Duck-billed dinosaurs! These animals lived in many places in the prehistoric world. Find out how they survived millions of years ago and what they have in common with today's animals.

DUCK-BILLED DINOSAURS

Dinosaurs lived between 230 million and 65 million years ago. There were many different kinds of dinosaurs. The duck-billed dinosaur had a wide, flat beak, like that of a duck. Some duck-billed dinosaurs had a crest on their heads. They all ate plants and lived at the end of the age of dinosaurs.

Deep in a forest, three herds of different duck-billed dinosaurs lived together. *Charonosaurus, Lambeosaurus,* and *Corythosaurus* all had different head crests. The crests may have helped them tell each other apart.

Tsintaosaurus lived in what is now China. On the top of its head was a crest that looked like a spike. The spike was a long, thin bone that stuck straight up. It was hollow like a tube. Perhaps *Tsintaosaurus* blew air through this special bone to make noises.

Crested heads today

The hornbill bird has a crest, like *Tsintaosaurus* once had. The hornbill uses its crest to push branches out of the way so its bill can reach berries.

Size Comparison

Tsintaosaurus might have had a small piece of colorful skin joined to its head crest.

OLOROTITAN

Pronunciation:
oh-LAW-ro-TYE-tan

Olorotitan was a duck-billed dinosaur with a big, bony crest on the back of its head. The crest made the animal's head look much bigger than it really was. The crest also might have made *Olorotitan* look very dangerous to its enemies.

Big faces today

The frilled lizard of Australia can show a collar of skin around its neck. Like *Olorotitan*'s crest once did, the lizard's frill helps scare away other animals.

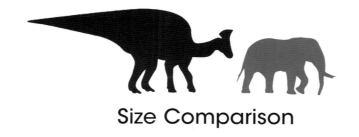

Size Comparison

8

Olorotitan's crest
was made up of the
bones of its nose.
It was shaped like
an ax.

9

Charonosaurus had a long crest made up of bony tubes. It could blow air from its nostrils through the tubes. This action could have made a trumpetlike noise. The noise may have been a call to other dinosaurs.

Noisy animals today

The modern howler monkey uses its lungs to make sounds that can be heard throughout the forest. The monkey makes its home a noisy place, much like *Charonosaurus* once did.

Size Comparison

Charonosaurus' crest may have been good for pushing through bushes, just like a snowplow pushes through snow.

Lambeosaurus had short front legs and low shoulders that allowed it to reach plants on the ground. The dinosaur used a wide, narrow beak to nip and chew the plants. When *Lambeosaurus* was not eating, it held its head up high so other dinosaurs could see its crest.

Low grazers today

The modern kangaroo hunches down to eat from the ground, just like *Lambeosaurus* once did.

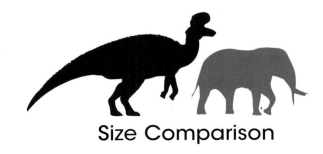

Size Comparison

The head crest of *Lambeosaurus* had a big square section in front and a little horn behind it.

CORYTHOSAURUS

Pronunciation:
kor-ith-o-SAW-rus

Corythosaurus, like many other duck-billed dinosaurs, nested with a herd. Year after year, it came back to the same nesting site to lay its eggs. Adults cared for their young until the young ones could look after themselves.

Nesting in groups

The modern flamingo nests with a large group, much like *Corythosaurus* did long ago.

Size Comparison

Corythosaurus made a small mound for a nest. Its young hatched from eggs that had been placed in a hollow section of the mound.

15

Shantungosaurus was one of the biggest duck-billed dinosaurs. It used its beak to scrape leaves and conifer needles from high tree branches. It used hundreds of teeth to chew its food.

Tree feeding today

The modern moose has a broad mouth. It also eats tough needles from conifer trees, just like *Shantungosaurus* once did.

Size Comparison

Shantungosaurus had a strong, sharp beak that was covered with bony material.

ORYCTODROMEUS

Pronunciation:
o-RIK-toe-DRO-ME-us

Oryctodromeus was a small duck-billed dinosaur. It had long fingers and strong shoulders that helped it burrow into the ground and form an underground den. Scientists recently found the bones of an *Oryctodromeus* family in North America.

Burrowing animals today

Like *Oryctodromeus* once did, the modern black bear makes an underground den in which to hide and to bring up young.

Size Comparison

Oryctodromeus stayed in or near the den, looking after its babies until they were ready to leave.

Saurolophus may have had a pouch of skin on top of its snout. If it blew air into the pouch, the pouch would have filled like a balloon. When *Saurolophus* snorted out the air, it probably made a noise.

Noisy pouches today

The modern frog has a pouch that it fills with air. When the frog blows out the air, it croaks. Perhaps *Saurolophus* sounded like a frog.

Size Comparison

The noise made by *Saurolophus* might have traveled a long way. This may have been how it talked to others in its group.

WHERE DID THEY GO?

Dinosaurs are extinct, which means that none of them are alive today. Scientists study rocks and fossils to find clues about what happened to dinosaurs.

People have different explanations about what happened. Some people think a huge asteroid that hit Earth caused all sorts of climate changes, which caused the dinosaurs to die. Others think volcanic eruptions caused the climate change and that killed the dinosaurs. No one knows for sure what happened to all of the dinosaurs.

GLOSSARY

beak—the hard front part of the mouth of birds and some dinosaurs; also known as a bill

conifer—trees that produce seeds in cones and have needlelike leaves

crest—a structure on top of the head, usually used to signal to other animals

duck-billed—to have a broad, flat beak or bill, like that of a duck

frill—a collar of hair, feathers, or bone that surrounds an animal's neck

hatched—broke out of an egg

herd—a large group of animals that moves, feeds, and sleeps together

nesting—to build or live in a nest

snout—the long front part of an animal's head, where its nose and jaws are located

spike—a sharp, pointed growth

TO LEARN MORE

MORE BOOKS TO READ

Clark, Neil, and William Lindsay. *1001 Facts About Dinosaurs.* New York: Dorling Kindersley, 2002.

Dixon, Dougal. *Dougal Dixon's Amazing Dinosaurs.* Honesdale, Penn.: Boyds Mills Press, 2007.

Holtz, Thomas R., and Michael Brett-Surman. *Jurassic Park Institute Dinosaur Field Guide.* New York: Random House, 2001.

ON THE WEB

FactHound offers a safe, fun way to find Web sites related to topics in this book. All of the sites on FactHound have been researched by our staff.

1. Visit *www.facthound.com*

2. Type in this special code: 1404840184

3. Click on the FETCH IT button.

Your trusty FactHound will fetch the best Web sites for you!

INDEX

LOOK FOR ALL OF THE BOOKS IN THE DINOSAUR FIND SERIES: